A TEMPORARY DWELLING

Jiwon Choi

SPUYTEN DUYVIL
NEW YORK CITY

© 2024 Jiwon Choi
ISBN 978-1-959556-88-6
Cover Art: "Stroll" by Barbara Friedman
barbarafriedmanpaintings.com

Library of Congress Control Number: 2023949711

In memory of my beloved aunt, Hwang Soon Hee
(May 9, 1931-July 8, 2020)

"...our worldly flesh is nothing more than a temporary dwelling."

—Haruki Murakami

Contents

I.

II

A TEMPORARY DWELLING

I

INSECT IN UTOPIA

I was told I could
be here
I could take off my shoes here
I was told I could roll my ball of dung
up the hill here
I was told I could toss my peanut shells
on the ground here
I was told I could choose which seven stages of grief
to undergo here
start my simple metamorphosis
and grow out of my sophomore exo-skeleton here
bypass the nymph and twee years
I was told I could rip the head off my mate here
I was told I will go through at least three sheddings
before achieving perfect symmetry here
my head impaled on to my thorax with an abdomen that lights up
at the mention of potato chips
especially the sour cream and onion kind
I was told no one will be jealous of me here
and that I will be taken seriously

I was told this is utopia.

CIVILIZATION

Sixteenth century Nicaragua a rabbit could be bought
for six beans of cacao
eight for a pig
a lady's fancy cost ten
what does this mean for a civilization
that built stairways to heaven with bare hands
and carried gods
on their shoulders?

Hands of your seven year old brother
skin tearing
legs of your pregnant sister
bones breaking
hearts of your last uncles
ligaments exploding
to get those mountains built
so we could be just next door
to mount olympus

in our stick houses
mixed up with mud and cow dung
goats sleeping in the corner
next to our kettle pot
leave the door open
so the angels may
come in.

Become Galaxies

scribbled notes
of pharaohs
fragments
of
legacy
papyrus
particles
floating in
the ionosphere
inhaled
by zeus
seconds
later
an explosion
of dust
to become
galaxies

100 DAYS

I made it

and my father ordered a large pepperoni
comes with a side of garlic knots
put out more coin for a molten lava
cake

did they just call me "hey"
on day one so I could at least turn
my big head to look at them?

these days I try not to look
at the guy on his crutch in front of
walgreens yelling "hey can you donate?"
then calling me a cheapskate
when I don't

well, I can be cheap
but cannot skate.

Vincent Chin, You Were Living the American Dream

I.

An arm band
a Star of David set up
or a sign around your neck
to define the parameters of you
not being from Japan
not made in Japan

of not being a Nissan, a Mazda
Mitsubishi
you are not a Honda

they would not admit to the mistake
would not admit to knowing there was a difference
can you tell the difference?

Vincent, you were living the American Dream
a dream two guys who worked in a Detroit auto factory jerry rigged for you

a dream
where they chase you in front of a McDonald's
and beat your head in

what do autoworkers who beat your head in want you to dream about?

you are not white in this dream
you are not allowed to be white
baseball bats can be white

what do baseball bats want you to dream about?

II.

Vincent, what kind of music do white autoworkers
who bludgeon you to death
listen to?

Don't tell me they listen to Bruce Springsteen
listen to Darkness on the Edge of Town on a loop
in the tape deck of their America First pick-up truck
on the way to the factory

it's the work   just the work   the working life

III.

Arrested and released the same night
driven home by his wife
what does a white autoworker who bludgeons you to death do
when he gets home? He eats dinner.
Slabs of middle America pot roast alongside boiled potatoes
and limp carrots his wife warms up
But no, of course he will call upon the Take Out gods
to allow him to order Chinese just this once
consider it his death row meal–General Tso's Chicken
pork lo mein and too many egg rolls to count
with extra hot mustard

a feast for this prodigal son
to choke on.

There Are Cats in Bags

I am in the back seat of a taxi
with my mom
there's a lady in the front with a brown shopping
bag full of cats
we all get out and the lady empties the bag
onto the sidewalk
it is night and it looks like we are near the park
where I go sledding
down hills on garbage can lids
during lunch recess
returning soaking wet socks
and canvas sneakers

there are cats in bags
passing through our lives.

HARBINGER

With a twisted nose and sorry mouth she is all
wallflower eating white bread with mayo

vigilant virgin at thirty
still believing you can wish someone dead

and no turning back from that
she works in a factory cutting beaks

off chickens, plucking their feathers
eager to reach the rubbery skin

secretly she knows she is growing her own feathers
and though she has gotten used to the smell of death

she cannot smell her own decomposing.

BODY MASS INDEX

I.

I am an only child who ate too much candy
like my father before me, my sweet tooth is both backfire
and source of power. I resemble how gaga my Father was
for Hershey bars
spawn and sprung from his frontal cerebral lobe
like Athena I go forth to pillage
half-off Halloween candy from all the supermarkets
of America

proclivities passed down
transcribed into molecules that make up
my body mass index

indexed in me are also the hankerings of my mother
a pop-up menu of her girlhood
then years as a wrathful housewife on West 107th Street

cold noodles in a light bean broth

      small red beans simmering with sweet rice dumplings

            thick cut bologna fried in butter, squished between white
            bread

(the kind of bread that reminds you of flesh off the backside or that resides
inner thigh).

II.

Our bodies are not catalogued with kindness
we become mere calculations of kilograms and inches
of fat parcels and skin flaps
our hocks and jowls
relegated to pig part-status
a tokenism of the jowl variety
not taken seriously for the genres and subgenres
we contribute
for instance our fetlocks
our knuckles of meat
our ankles for pickling

this proclivity for flesh is to be admired

do not dismiss me as merely a Happy Meal.

III.

And so nothing of the flesh will remain

our mothers and fathers go back to the everlasting
where do you think babies come from, anyway?

But then what is left?

Nothing but the air between us
as sweet as orange blossoms
which I must gulp
as if I am drowning
my body is sure we are
drowning

but if I am not drowning then it is the same feeling as waiting
for mountains to roll back
into the ocean
for trees to grow wings
and go where trees
will not get pissed on.

WHITE BREAD

I have become as soft as the loaf my mother brought home
from the Olympia Supermarket (107th Street
 & Broadway) tender dough of her loins
look at me
I am flesh rising and falling
a yeasty round for you
to pull apart

we are white bread sandwiches
everyday bologna and government cheese
a death mask pressed
into the holes of my eyes
I won't stop until I have filled all the black spaces
of my face
like Frankenstein's monster
my mortal skin
is rigor mortis

and limbs sewn to reassemble
a human-ness

a petrified forest
of organs

I am processed trauma.

I Want to Get Out of My Body

"...the vista includes only the displacement of feeling back
into the body, which gave birth to the feelings that don't
sit comfortably inside the communal."
                    —Claudia Rankine

When I unhinge the hinge that fastens my head
to my neck
to let it lapse and nestle into folds of skin
I will rival the most wet equations
of flour egg   milk   butter
forget babka and challah
mantou got nothing
on me

watch
don't look
away

watch as
I reveal:
my kitchen sink
of all the red beans   and spinach
not broken
down

here are the insides
of me
spilling out
on to the sidewalk next to gum wrappers

and ghostly dryer sheets
heaps of skin

              from rubbery chicken

that cannot be melted
by my gastric effort

my chemical reactions
cannot make
head or tail
hoof or snout
foot or mouth
out of any of it.

It's time to get out of my body.

Process Trauma

I could count a hundred pounds
by the time I was 8
the more I ate the more I could see
I was free and
if I'm going to die
I am ready to lasso my heartbreak
to a cheesecake

pass the eggs and bacon in between pancakes
spaghetti on top of cheesy bread
will be my end

but chili, hamburger and fries
a joyful breaking point
with a suicide by Family Meal:

sixteen-piece chicken bucket
hush puppies bolstered
with a pile of onion rings

my bed flew out the back
of the pick-up
chasing down the Good Humor man
outside Chicago

two dollars left
in my pocket
can I get a chocolate
eclair
with that?

If You Don't Have a Car to Drive to Whole Foods Supermarket

The family of rats moved in
next door
keep to themselves
mostly Papa Rat hangs out
on the fire escape gnawing
a chicken wing or cherry tomato
while Mama stays inside
keeping babies one through five
in line
what does she think about the online
learning mandated by the mayor
in this cluster of zip codes
by the border?

How's their wi-fi?

Do these new neighbors look like they might
knock on our door to borrow
a cup of sugar or bottle of rum—you know
for flambé? Hard to say
but I will be ready with a bowl
of fuck off and cup of
"we're not home."

II

WHAT THE GODS BEQUEATH US

for Louise Bogan

By four years old you knew
your Wednesday schedule walking
with your mother through dim hallways
leading to hotel beds and random men

you wouldn't always remember the wallpaper
but seeing your mother's fisted hand on a pillow
is probably what blinded you
for two days

and as far as epiphany goes
you have known for some time that the gods
made you out of glass
so you would not shatter
just become full of cracks.

KOREAN BREAKFAST

is the mourning process
of losing a mother
and puzzling over a hieroglyphic system
of lines falling into single and double
horizontal and vertical formation
with an occasional ο (yes, like "oh")
wedged in
to create characters
(yes, like in a story)
that tell me how to prepare fern bracken
and sweet potato stems
or mi-na-ri

but neither the mourning brain nor morning mouth take charge
leaving it to the night stomach to set diligent
rations of hot rice, fried egg
and our ancestral cabbage
co-opted to an inch
of her leaf

say, how about you take back your spam
and no hard feelings?

Otherwise, have you met my friend
crested warty cabbage?

May Tenth, Two Thousand Twenty: Will an Asterisk Be Added?

Of the eighteen thousand two hundred days I have been here
what parcel will be deemed most productive?
In the ledger of paying keen attention
what days will be proclaimed least
riddled with tomfoolery?

For sure, it will be the Mother's Day my mother died

will an asterisk be added?

But then will the days she thought I was someone else due to
early onset dementia be factored in?

And will there be an indication that she liked being a mother
having chosen to be and not succumbed into the expectation
of women using their uterus
of women enduring the vagaries of men.

Of men who are the male of our species
and not exactly counterparts
or even opposites

though I have seen the term 'appendage' used once or twice

will an asterisk be added?

At my mother's age now, I have let my own uterus off
the hook
entering into disuse

I have become a place people call *barren*
as if they'd wandered into an expanse of burned down
buildings and trees

but it's just here
where I've been
today, tomorrow, and yesterday
in a tally of unknowable days

will an asterisk be added?

Forever Schedule

We the living
have this compulsion:
walk into the past, as if the past
has been waiting at the kitchen table
for our return
but this is not Pompeii
and we do not have to embody a petrified forest
of daily life
of decorating the cake, dismantling the pig
of washing your husband's loin cloth
(even here there's no getting those stains out)
present becomes forever
but the past must go on
organizing the forever schedule
sorting and erasing memories
for how quickly these get hoarded
into current events
and we the living cannot grasp
this concept all the while piles under beds
molder and the collection of supermarket bags
dangling from door knobs begs forgiveness
of all who walk by
and brush up against all the plastic
pretentiousness
of these sad sacks.

DEMAND A BETTER ENDING

The last time I will admit to having passion
is the last time I tried to distract Tragedy
with a joke about the Pope getting pulled over
for speeding, but Tragedy like a brown mouse
does not have a sense of humor
and knows where you live
caring only about finding your millet
cache.

And then there's the time Tragedy appeared to me
as the boy I loved: yellow hair and eyes like a dove
for whom I packed meat and bread every morning
ironing creases into his pants
the way he liked and no one said anything about getting
used to sour milk and leaking cups
and no one said anything about the boy you love
taking your meat and bread one day
and never coming back.

So Tragedy becomes our failure to read the room
to parse destiny from luck, mistaking
the kicking in of our teeth as a sign
of good things to come

but these confessions
are best reserved for the fortune teller next door
foreshadowing Tragedy pulling up to the curb
where she'll sort and catalog us
for kidnapping
ebola virus
Jehovah's witness

so have your Saturday Night Special handy
and demand a better ending
how about something ironic or romantic?

Yes to metaphysical.

I Am Not a Secret, You Must Admire Me

I know about gravity
must speak truth about our place
on the Periodic Table next to
inert gasses and metabolic
solutions

we are still trying to lasso the sun
while filling prescriptions for bigger gonads
with pangolins
the kind of lazy philosophy that will land us
on the shelf of leftovers
next to old milk and sweaty hot dogs

the Ancients at the ready with their hemlock
come the slightest whiff of heresy
but happy we are with sloppy truth
squandering nuance with random drive-by
readings of Wikipedia
pages upon pages bleeding
revisions

in this game of can't-tell-the difference-between-truth-
and-falsehood
there is no more room at the inn.

POET OF THE SITUATION

You catch me up in the cloak of the good
daughter
send me off to cross
thresholds
into rooms of the aggrieved and noisy
whose floors are resolutely dank
forever carpeted
with beer
and spittle

even Agamemnon
ten years at war
a stranger to his own
house
got the red carpet treatment
upon his return

and how many thresholds did he curse
clutching his rage that became the bloom
of a sacrifice he had no right
to make

is this us every time we walk into a room
we do not know?
reluctantly becoming the poet of the situation
embodying
a dramatic monologue
in someone else's keg party-cum
-screenplay?

Agamemnon who could recite the words to begat
blood
learned in the wrath of gods
counting out feet to measure war
as pleasure—our original weird
poet

but we're all weird poets now
rewriting scenes to our liking
because we cannot say what's the matter
when it matters.

But you won't win the lottery
just because you write a sonnet
about it.

Instar is Not Existence

Sad exoskeleton
goes to a ridiculously liberal arts college
in Vermont
and ends up using two of her seven
moltings
entomologists say
are necessary to achieve
symmetry
for antennae, fangs
and other extremities
to emerge
as pleasing

but am willing
to use up more
if a protactinium
existence
is in the cards
bring on my alchemic
intervention.

BEAUTIFUL MUTANT

In Rochester of 1992
after a dinner of spaghetti
in red sauce
we went to a bar
where I became a pygmy
under glass
where I was made to Ota Benga
myself into a beautiful
mutant

no rope was thrown
to capture me
I was simply surrounded
by men who frequent bars
in gangs
in groups
in mobs
to make a point
about ownership.

Oh, to be a beautiful mutant
in America
among the wilted people
stuck in their time
like that girl in Little Rock
whose face is frozen
in forever
but still twitching hate

her digitized face will outlast the Pharaohs
not even time erases rage lines
or reconciles the angry gash
as mouth

how much she must have loved walking
down this pansy path
of entitlement
in an incidental town
where she learned to gloat
about birthright
in a town that didn't understand: separate water fountains
is a dick move.

Oh, tattered town, dick town of
America
you serve the weakest red sauce
you'd think it was pink

this side of the Mason Dixon.

What Do You Not Want to Know

"We were not lying about what happened in Tulsa."
Kalalea, NPR

What do you not want to know
about the burning of houses
in a town in Oklahoma
with someone's grandmother still inside
she was in the middle of setting potatoes
and chicken necks into a skillet
like she does every sundown

what do you not want to know
about fire bombing a town
from the sky
because it could not be taken
from the ground

the burning bodies
outside of a house used for target practice
will always be there
no matter how many pages
you tear out of a textbook

if school children in Japan
are allowed to read about the piles of tongues cut
out of mouths alongside piles
of ears then maybe
we can all stop flying
into windows like the birds
who don't know
what a window is.

Bollocks

The opinions in this piece are solely that of the poet.
No British musicians were deified in the writing of this poem.

I. Fame

This idea
coming out of your ears
and arse
the need to believe
you can fly

you are an algorithm
of privilege and desire
shooting down the sun with
your terrible ambition
claiming you discovered gold
becoming the slick mimic
a coyote jester
without charm.

II. Responsibility

Ships in utero
birthing bodies
hearts dying.

Are you the first
in your family
to love a black person?

Congratulations.

III. Fred

You used to cut my hair
in your East Village apartment

but when I called Clapton
bargain basement
Blues
you gave me bangs.

Gee, thanks.

IV. Elvis 2.0

Your drunken slander
printed on paper
is all we remember

Elvis Costello
hearts
Ray Charles.

WATCHING *PLATOON* ON NEW YEAR'S DAY 2020

you're okay
with your voyeurism
watching black and white
men kill the yellow
man

yes, I mean
the scenes of gratuitous
jungle violence where you
imagine
you are a soldier in the thicket
shooting off
your automatic weapon
because you have
been authorized
by every lyndon, dick and henry
to kill yellow
people

diem if you do, diem if you
don't.

The Child of Immigrants

Nineteen-nineties Alfonse D'amato
hell bent performative idiot of his tribe
tribal is what he made it
he played his Italian-ese on tv for the people watching tv
to a city that sometimes thinks the immigrants
are not them
but okay, yes their grandfather, not them
but okay, yes, Uncle Gianni from Siena Bologna Forli

did you say Fort Lee? Isn't that all Korean?

Who are you calling foreign
what's wrong with being foreign

the child of immigrants always wanting to tell the truth
but not in prose
don't want to write prose
writing fiction is like having to eat a whole chicken
when you just need a wing or thigh
or even the butt would do

do you see how the stranger gets caught in the dragnet
dragged through the town square
rope taut pulled to cut
off air and hope

in other words, if you call me
a mutant, know that I am also
a bitch.

Kill the Bitch and You Eliminate the Litter

Pinochet,
are you saying it will take decades for us
to get out of the pumpkin patch
if ever?
You got to go home
ailing from years of counting all those fingernails
pulled off dissidents
students and teachers,
farmers really
children of the revolution who didn't
agree with your economics
of one man rule
and three hundred percent inflation.
It's hard to agree
isn't it?
It's a wonder bread gets buttered
even on the one side
you didn't want to argue about why
ketchup on hot dogs was a moral trespass
so rather
you put everyone in a stadium
disappearing the contradictions
was your specialty

and here come the men in suits to put quarters in
the everlasting cycle of dirty cash
called international banking

while all you can do is be a carcass plugged full
of dirt and worms
while all I can do is keep looking for skillet chicken
recipes online.

THE ONLY JOSEON* GIRL HERE

I am not the last of my kind but the only Joseon girl
here
the only one you rolled up in an army blanket and left
to unfurl
in this three-mule beer cozy town where every backroom comes with
a family of dormice
ensconced behind the stove, working for hot dog wages at gas stations
and bodegas all over town.
Optimism is how I find the wormhole for quantum leaping out of your
life
you will tell my mother I was ungrateful and insist she pay the cable
bill
you will claim to the local news that I was a slut because I drank gin
and shaved my legs
but the simple truth (not truthy enough for you) is that this world was
too greedy for me.

*Joseon, the last dynastic Korean kingdom, 1392-1897.

St. Anne Delivers the First Devil

My body is a grave
for my unborn child
he will come out of me
already dead or he will be
a ghost

I take after my mother
she was full of dark places
distant but interested in parties
and gentlemen callers

I tried to kill myself when I was 28
I had two kids by then and my husband was on the road
a lot
we eloped when I was eighteen
he was nineteen, studying to be a doctor
dropped out of school to become a salesman of wool
so he could take care of me
and our baby

I didn't know I could stop being a baby machine
stop making
babies for you
because I had become just udders
and teats

here are the demons of my childhood
men as wife beaters and whore chasers
women as whore chasers and baby beaters
we are at the mercy of broken adults

and I have become a demon
from my own poison womb
my own rotten flesh sewn together
like Frankenstein's child

I will deliver the first devil.

III

Sonny Stitt Plays Bird

for Dick Lourie

sonny stitt
plays now's the time
and you believe you can fly
believe you have discovered the magic flute
to propel you, cut through this tightened seal of time and space
you can traverse the complications of your
diminution here
what your imagination will not allow
your body memory will thereby realize
you were of wings after all
riding the north wind
across these hemispheres
making the seasons

guadalajara
lima
saginaw
detroit

come
embody
light.

Ritual

John Coltrane
plugging and rolling
paper
with that good
tobacco

expert of ritual
working thumb and index
in a practice
of making

satisfaction with hands

working thumb and index
in meditation

in a practice
of setting an ancient plant
on fire

before setting the world
on fire.

Angels and Barbeque on Fourth Avenue

Rub the pig with brown sugar—
that's how to make it brown
and sweet and how you'd get it
in Memphis: a rack and quart
of beer eased in under your belt
alongside the bourbon and lime
in a tall glass.

Tonight the sky breaks into a dance
of electricity as angels alight
on Fourth Avenue. Believe in
wings, they are not overrated,
they are a miracle.

You say angels and barbeque
impose too much on poetic license
but I say angels on Fourth Avenue in their sturdy tweed
and no-nonsense footwear is just what you
would expect with a side order
of wings.

SITTING UNDER THE LAST COIN TELEPHONE MACHINE ON FIFTH AVENUE, BROOKLYN

In the laundromat
across from the taco take-out
next to the last Polish deli market
I contemplate the meaning of life
in the presence of possibly the last coin
telephone machine in Brooklyn

my life in fabrics and apparel—
blue towel, black bra and panties tumbling
until they are swallowed and spat out
by bright yellow sheets.   What do these cottons
and polyester blends cycling in time
say about our mortal existence?

I am seeking answers even Hegel and Julia Child would
not conjure
though I believe in art as a mode of being
and scrambling perfect eggs is essential for that mode
no one can say Poseidon isn't reclaiming Venice
or that Zeus on a whim won't unplug the Aurora
Borealis to bring us back
to darkness

which reminds me of the last time I saw my father
fighting insomnia in a hospital tv room
where televisions were turned off by eleven.
He was staring at the grey screen
as if waiting for a signal
from beyond
I don't mean the grave
but outer space.

GOOD CROWS

for Jon of the Crows

Here are the birds, for certain crows, who ken first
when Death is near
perhaps the reaper of souls' way of sending advance
notice, a speed dial from the Other Side

do we say it is so because crows are the most boisterous?

But what about us, the blue jays will insert.

What about them, indeed?
Watch them work to impress upon you their glorious ruckus
no matter who's awake or not
and you will be tempted to agree
but no, they are too cheerful in their blue tuxedos and mullet
top hats, too charming in their flight of jaunty
cacophony

they are no harbingers of sorrow.

Good crows, thank you for your signal for us to take our last breath
before we get stamped

RETURN TO SENDER.

BEAUTIFUL FOREVER

hooked up
to a machine
to make you breath for a month
that is how delicate you became
how transparent your skin
stretched to invisibility
your dark blue veins
traveling above ground
arteries of water on land mass
you looked like a map

THE MOTH IN YOUR KITCHEN

could be your mother
come back to see you
your mother who died
last year in the hospital
where you asked the doctor to send
you a picture of her
and he did send
a picture you can not show anyone
for the horror of it
like in the Werner Herzog movie
when he warns the lady not to
listen to
the recording of the Grizzly Man
and his girlfriend being eaten alive
by a bear

but what if the mosquito you just smacked
against your leg at the cemetery
in between looking and listening for birds
by the dell was really
your mother

some god's bad joke
about karma?

but really she must have been the blue heron
suddenly seen
up to her knees and bill
in the water
stabbing at fish

so in your head the conversation goes
"Pardon me, by chance are you
the reincarnation of my mother, a tall Korean woman
who married a short dentist?"
But you don't feel anything
you who believe in signs
who looks for signs
who dreams in signs.

She is the sign
isn't she?

Not the Muse I Asked For

I write when I'm hungry
when I'm sour
I wish for the muse of Sappho
to take over
from my muse who is not the muse
I asked for
he is the muse who came with the all-night
deli across the street
clutching his malt liquor
whilst unleashing his dirge
a siren song masquerading as epiphany
is just bleating
inevitability

I could have sworn I asked for a muse
who could find God
lost somewhere in the constant
rhyme
of ancient urns
relapsed in the invisible ink
of ancient drums

sans muse I must write God into my life
by savoring the unruly honeysuckle
eating all the bread and drinking all
the wine
as I cry for Cabiria and her nights
when Fellini comes
to town.

WOEBEGONE IN THE GOURMET DELI
ACROSS THE STREET FROM LINCOLN CENTER

Missing some upfront teeth
in a stained possibly London Fog-Burberry (still don't know the difference)
raincoat, her hair never looks washed
orders the same two dollars worth of curry chicken salad
and two slices of prosciutto, denouement with a slab of key lime pie
all the days we're behind the counter snickering and disgusted but afraid.
We do and don't know we will end up the same
we are the front of house but should have been in the back.

The whispers are that she's an heiress gone mad
looney tunes on Columbus Avenue.

If Aretha Franklin Talked
About Being Interested in a Man

It could have been during an interview when a reporter
brought up the topic
but what could she say, really
this being National Television and all?
So she recounted instead the time she saw Charlie Mingus
slap a piano player across the head
to get his attention.

An allegory?

Or how they did it in the olden days
but who said she was looking?

Plan Queen Bee coming up:
muster your best Rodgers and Hart
and conjure the maiden's prayer:

glad to be unhappy
alone and at sea
a ship without a sail

knowing her heart was full
but her arms were too short to box
with God

and no one in TV Land
blinked.

THE WORLD IN A JAR

remember those kids in sunset park
missionaries
mormon white shirts
trying to convert the masses
in this case old chinese women
pulling their carts laden with persimmon
and globes of purple grapes
their perfect cantonese beguiling
especially when they get to the part about
being reborn on your own planet
sure, dedicate the whole day, the whole year
eating as many grapes as you can
no one will yell at you when you spit out all those seeds
all over the galaxies
why, what a vision: millions of vines hanging
and grapes ready for the plucking
just as god intended.

COLLISION

sparrow kamikazes
into spokes spinning to eternity
final thought: asphalt

BOBOLINK

Take my heart into your mouth
    as you would
      a lemon
        sour

roll it on your tongue and let it
    excite you, over-
      flowing the
        cavern

of your mouth with the life
    you remember as
      a black
        bird

or was it a bobolink? Gathering
    in rice fields to eat up
      the sweet
        rice.

Each grain you pluck thinking
    nothing of the end
      of harvest, or
        the fall

of market prices. I can see you
    then as you are now
      a sprite
        creature

singing a joyous gurgle
with a mouth
full of
spume.

Epilogue

CONTEMPLATE MOUNTAINS
(Greene County, New York)

Spiders have taken all night
to spin webs
in the middle of this rough road
we are not their first choice
but get snared just the same

when I stumble over rocks
it is how I contemplate mountains
churning and shrugging off boulders
as blithely as a tree would shake off
leaves
the land changing its mind
shifting keeps shifting
in witness of creatures made to resemble
lichen and moss
inertia as action
as the Eastern Bluebirds escape
their fossil identities
to summon winds
from the east
the north
and the sea

worthy muses
breathing into us
the light of
the world.

HERE'S THE MISSISSIPPI

You grew up not knowing about oceans
satisfied with what came out of the faucet—
water beyond does not occur
to you

water a billion years old
dripping down the caves of Johannesburg

maybe from Mars?

The search for life in the rocks will stop
when they find the fossil remains of us
saying we are predominantly salt and not
much more than single cell
organisms

and here's the Mississippi
going back to the beginning

so get your house out of the way.

A Temporary Dwelling

Does the spider who hitches a ride
on our rental car in front of the rental toilet
adjacent the hiking trail know she is on a car
and not a dinosaur?

She has discovered new territory
and must recalibrate how to proceed

not so the warbler crashed into the glass
door of our rented house in the woods
ending her calculation here
with wings the color of ferns that flicker and beckon
bluffside forever suspended
in last flight

in our world of perfect time
she found a way to stop it.

ACKNOWLEDGEMENTS

The Banyan Review: "Insect in Utopia"
Hanging Loose: "White Bread"; "Sonny Stitt Plays Bird"; "Angels and Barbeque on Fourth Avenue"; "Bobolink"; "Here's the Mississippi"; "Vincent Chin, You Were Living the American Dream"; "If Aretha Franklin Talked About Being Interested in a Man": "Beautiful Mutant"
Heavy Feather Review: "What Don't You Want to Know"; "There Are Cats in Bags" *West Trestle Review*: "Contemplate Mountains"

Jɪwon Choɪ is a poet, early childhood educator, and urban gardener. She is the author of two poetry collections, *One Daughter is Worth Ten Sons* and *I Used To Be Korean*. Choi started her community garden's first poetry reading series, *Poets Read in the Garden*, during the early Covid years to support local writers. You can find out more about her at iusedtobekorean.com.

www.ingramcontent.com/pod-product-compliance
Lightning Source LLC
Chambersburg PA
CBHW031228120626
46545CB00003B/1041